Fairies at Bedtime

Fairies at Bedtime

Tales of Inspiration and Delight for You to Read
with Your Child – to Enchant, Comfort and Enlighten

WATKINS PUBLISHING

LONDON

Fairies at Bedtime

First published in the United Kingdom and Ireland in 2012 by
Watkins Publishing, an imprint of Duncan Baird Publishers
Sixth Floor, Castle House
75–76 Wells Street
London W1T 3QH

Conceived, created and designed by Duncan Baird Publishers

Managing Editor: Sandra Rigby
Senior Editor: Fiona Robertson
Managing Designer: Suzanne Tuhrim
Commissioned Artwork: Fei

British Library Cataloguing-in-Publication Data:
A CIP record for this book is available from the British Library

ISBN: 978-1-78028-385-2

10 9 8 7 6 5 4 3 2 1

Typeset in Filosofia
Colour reproduction by XY Digital
Printed in China by Imago

A NOTE ON GENDER
In sections of this book intended for parents, to avoid burdening the reader repeatedly with
phrases such as "he or she", "he" and "she" are used alternately, topic by topic, to refer to a child.

Contents

About This Book

Welcome to the magical world of fairies — a world where nature is alive with spirits and sprites, by turns shy or playful, thoughtful or mischievous, but always ready to share their world with humans, if we only take the time to look around us.

Reading these stories with your child will help both of you come to a deeper appreciation of the natural world — the domain of fairies. From the dryads or tree spirits of ancient Greece and Rome to the elves of Scandinavian tradition, and from the *devas* of Hinduism to the *kami* or nature spirits of traditional Japanese Shintoism, the idea that nature is a place rich in spiritual energy that must be honoured has been important in many cultures until recent times. Today, we are growing ever more concerned about protecting our environment. This book embodies the principles of learning to respect nature, tuning into its rhythms and appreciating its beauty, so that the next generation can live more harmoniously within the world than our own.

However, these stories are not just about the natural world. *Fairies at Bedtime* is also concerned with the daily experiences of your child and offers insights and assistance into the handling of her ordinary concerns – school, family, making friends, settling into a new home and so on. These are the issues that loom large in a child's life, and at times can cause anxiety. The message of the stories in this collection is that positive attitudes and a calm approach can make all kinds of challenges manageable. Together, you and your child can identify with the wonderful characters you will discover, and draw out themes and ideas to help make sense of the greater world. Your child's imagination and creativity, and her empathy and understanding, will all be strengthened.

This collection is perfect for reading aloud at bedtime, and of course children will also enjoy reading the stories themselves, The tales are designed to appeal to children between the ages of five and eight – although this is only a suggested age range. The magic of fairies can speak to a wide age group. Most importantly, you and your child will delight in sharing a stimulating, captivating and charming world – entering the realm of fairies will help both of you to see your everyday world through fresh and enlightened eyes.

What Are Fairies?

Fairies go by different names around the world and appear in a variety of forms, but the classic idea of the fairy as a tiny winged creature, often in a dress and cap made from flower petals or leaves, has been fixed in our imagination by artists from the 19th and early 20th centuries. Although human in form, these fairies were clearly shown to be very much part of the natural world. Artists illustrated them making their homes in bird nests, for example, or swinging on spiders' webs. They are shown peeping out of flowerheads or riding a ladybird just as a human might ride a horse.

The idea of spirits or energies that generally take on a miniature human form, but are an integral part of nature and not of the ordinary human world, is found in every culture around the world. In societies that live a life closely connected to nature, such as nomadic communities, nature spirits are still considered to be actively powerful. In recent years many people living in industrialized societies have become keen to understand and connect with nature and to try to "see" fairies and nature spirits in the way that our ancestors sensed their presence.

In the late 20th century a small community began
working with nature spirits at a remote caravan site at
Findhorn Bay in Scotland. Dorothy Maclean and her friends
Eileen and Peter Caddy sensed the presence of nature
spirits at the site and received the message that these
entities could help them produce a flourishing garden in
an unpromising, apparently barren setting. The garden at
Findhorn did indeed flourish and showed that co-operation
between humans and the natural world could occur under
very different terms to the techniques used in modern
agriculture. A sensitive awareness of the subtle energies at
work in the environment could lead to both productivity
and harmony.

The following pages briefly introduce fairy traditions
from around the world. Some of the fairies may sound
rather different to the tiny winged creatures you may
be most familiar with, but fairies can take many
forms. The wealth of folklore means that it has not
been possible to explore stories from every culture.
If you and your child would like to learn more, some
books about fairy folklore are suggested on page 140.

Celtic Fairies

A rich fairy tradition exists in the folklore of Ireland, Scotland, Wales and Brittany – what we think of as the Celtic countries. The poet W.B. Yeats collected and recorded many Irish folklore traditions and we owe much of our understanding of traditional fairy beliefs to his work.

Ireland was, it was believed, originally populated by a race of magical beings known as the Tuatha dé Danann, who came from another realm or Otherworld. These "fair folk" were blessed with extraordinary powers, lived in ancient barrows or cairns and would only rarely appear to ordinary mortals. Sometimes humans might be enticed to enter the realm of the fair folk, to find that time passed much more slowly there than in the world of humans. It was said that a month in fairyland might equal 100 human years.

Yeats described many strongly held beliefs about fairies, including the respect given to fairy paths – narrow trails appearing suddenly in the landscape and disappearing just as abruptly. Such pathways were considered to be a point of contact between our world and that of the fairies and it was considered very bad luck to interfere with them; so much so

that even in relatively recent times houses would not
be constructed on top of known fairy trails, and new
roads would be built to skirt around them.

Celtic tradition records the phenomenon of the
fairy procession, known in Scotland as the Fairy Rade
and in Wales as the Wild Hunt. This was a grand
cavalcade of fairies, often parading behind their king
and queen, which commonly travelled along fairy paths.
Only a few lucky mortals are said to have witnessed a
fairy procession.

Fairies are considered to be very fond of music, and fine
mortal musicians were held to be at risk of being spirited
away to the Otherworld to play their instruments for the
amusement of the fairy folk. Fairies were often reported
to have been seen dancing in circles, and it is said that
favoured and sensitive people can hear fairy music if they
listen carefully in wild places.

One of the most famous of Irish fairies is the leprechaun,
a solitary male fairy only 3 feet or 1 metre in height and
renowned for hoarding treasure. Leprechauns are generally
clad in green and are great shoemakers, often to be found

industriously hammering away at the sole of a tiny shoe. A human coming across a leprechaun may discover a great fortune in gold, but leprechauns have always to be approached with great caution for they are also famous for being bad-tempered.

Another important Irish fairy is the *leanan sidhe*, a spirit of the air who can bring with her creativity and inspiration. As ever in the world of the fairies, it is important not to abuse a gift. Many tales of the *leanan sidhe* record that although she offers inspiration to artists and poets, they may be called upon to sacrifice their time in the human world in order to devote themselves to her realm.

The *gwargedd annwn* are beautiful Welsh water sprites, slender with long blonde hair. Many mortal men fall in love with these sprites, but only if the suitors are good and kind can they can win the love of the *gwargedd annwn*. There are tales of *gwargedd annwn* marrying mortal men only to return to their watery home when they were treated unkindly. One of the most famous of the *gwargedd annwn* was the Lady of the Lake of Arthurian legend. She bestowed the magical sword Excalibur upon King Arthur, lifting it up and handing to him from beneath the dark waters of the lake.

Scottish traditions tell us of the selkies, creatures who live as seals in the sea but can shed their seal skins on dry land to emerge as beautiful women. Many legends describe mortal men trying to marry selkies by stealing their skins and compelling them to remain in the earthly realm. The moral of all these stories is that such alliances are doomed to failure – the wild selkie must be allowed to be true to her nature and return to her own environment.

In the Scottish Highlands, the *ceasg* was a mermaid who would grant three wishes to whoever managed to catch her. In common with the selkie, the *ceasg* would sometimes decide to marry a human. Scottish fairies from the Borders region include the habetrot, said to be the patron of spinning, and the silky, whose rustling silk garments were reputed to terrify household servants in bygone days as they went about their domestic chores.

Fairies of Earth, Air and Fire

Fairies are often categorized according to the element in which they dwell — the *gwargedd annwn* and selkies belong to the element of water, for example. In many countries, important fairies also belong to the elements of earth, fire and air.

German and Scandinavian countries are rich with traditions of earth fairies or dwarfs — creatures who inhabit caves and mines, often guarding a treasure of precious stones and gold. Although dwarfs have a reputation for grumpiness, they can be helpful and are considered wise, sometimes even having the ability to tell the future. Norse legend tells how dwarfs helped to spare the mischievous god Loki from the wrath of Thor. Thinking it was a great joke, Loki cut off the beautiful golden hair of Thor's wife, Sir. The clever dwarfs created hair of pure beaten gold for Sir, so that no one could tell that it was not her own. Dwarfs were famous for their skill in metal work and sword-making and were believed to dwell in magnificent halls lined with precious stones.

Other traditions tell of helpful earth fairies who assisted miners in their work. According to Cornish folklore, friendly fairies in the tin mines would knock to let miners know exactly where the richest veins of minerals could be discovered.

In Slavic countries, an air fairy is known as a *vila* or *wili*. These magical beings were believed to dwell throughout the natural world. Often taking the form of a beautiful woman, dressed in white and with long, flowing hair, a *vila* could also shape-shift, becoming a swan, a horse or a bird. The *vila* has a spellbinding voice and a mortal who hears her sing can forget to sleep, eat or drink for days.

The Hopi and Pueblo Native American cultures have tales of *kachinas*, spirits appearing in the clouds and stars, in lightning or the wind. *Kachinas* were greatly revered for their ability to teach humans important skills and can bring rainfall, promote healing and encourage fertility. *Kachinas* are present in our world from midwinter to midsummer, spending the rest of the year in their spirit world. Children were traditionally given *kachina* dolls that were believed to help impart spiritual knowledge to the young.

Tree Spirits

Trees have held special significance in many cultures as the home of wise and important spirits. In Native American traditions, trees are known as the Standing People and were revered for their great wisdom. The Cherokee people honoured the cedar in particular and believed that the spirits of their ancestors lived in that tree. The Cherokee traditionally carried a piece of cedar wood in a medicine bag for protection against evil spirits.

In Celtic tradition the oak, ash and thorn were termed the Fairy Triad and signalled the presence of fairies wherever they grew. Oak trees were accorded special respect and significant oaks were once carved with a protective circle which, it was believed, would help to prevent the trees being felled by either man or nature.

The oak is recognized as the king of trees in many cultures. In Greek mythology dryads were tree nymphs, and were originally believed to dwell in oak trees although over time their presence was extended to other tree species. Dryads were extremely shy creatures who rarely revealed themselves to humans; nevertheless they, and the oak trees in which they lived, were greatly honoured — according to the ancient Greek historian, Herodotus, the sacred oak grove at Dodona was recognized far and wide for its gift of prophecy. Hamadryads were especially long-lived tree spirits, but would die if their tree was felled. It was considered vital to first ask permission of an oak tree before damaging it in any way, in order to avoid the wrath of the gods.

In Japanese tradition it was believed to be extremely unlucky to fell a tree within which a *kodama* or tree spirit dwelled. "Spirit trees" were marked with a rope in order to identify and protect them.

In many traditions trees were considered to be a conduit between our world and the spirit realm. The World Tree is a symbol found in the mythology of many cultures, from the Norse to the Hindu, and features a tree as bridge between our world and the underworld and the heavens. In Scandinavian mythology, for example, Yggdrasil is an immense ash tree with branches extending far into the heavens and roots penetrating deep into the other realms.

The Power of the Imagination

These bedtime stories have been written with the aim of encouraging your child to relax into a calm state that will lead him to have a refreshing night's sleep. Each story opens with a paragraph that utilizes the techniques of visualization to help your child enter the story: to relax, empty his mind and imagine himself in a wood, by the sea or wherever the story is set. Creating a picture in his mind is an important way in which your child can develop the power of his imagination, and it will give him a sense of control over his thinking.

Visualization is a simple form of meditation that can be particularly appealing to children. It will help them to develop their imagination and empathy, as well as their problem-solving skills. By encouraging your child to build his own unique picture of the action of the story, you are teaching him how to detach from his daily concerns and explore new possibilities, people, places and adventures. He might feel inspired to draw or paint scenes from the tale or take it further, telling the on-going adventures of the characters. This will not only assist in nurturing your child's creativity and self-expression, but will also build his ability to see the viewpoint of others and to empathize with their problems and issues.

To check whether your child is able to visualize a scene – for example, the field of flowers in "The Fidget Fairy" (see page 56) – ask him to describe what he sees in his mind's eye. If your child seems to be having trouble, get him to close his eyes and ask some guided questions such as, "What colour is the sky?", "What plants can you see?", "Can you hear insects going about their business?" To help further develop your child's powers of imagination and concentration, try the visualization meditations on pages 136–9, written specifically for children. The more they practise, the easier it will be for them to paint their own pictures of stories that they encounter in the future.

Reading stories to children is one of the most effective ways to stimulate their imagination. The storyteller provides a framework on which the child's own imagination builds. The stories in this book are designed to excite without being overly prescriptive, allowing room for your child to fill in the gaps and explore further. Enjoy the process with your child.

Bedtime Reading

It may be difficult for children to relax at the end of the day. These stories about fairies are an excellent way to help your child to disengage from the challenges she has experienced, to wind down and slip peacefully into a gentle night's sleep.

You will probably need to prepare your child for a bedtime story so that she's in a positive and receptive frame of mind. Experts suggest that it's a good idea to use the same bedtime routine every evening — for example, dinner followed by a bath and then a story. Before you start reading try a quick relaxation exercise.

Ask your child to lie on her back on the bed and let her legs and arms gently sink into the mattress. Ask her to close her eyes and begin to take some deep breaths in and out. Tell her that with every breath she is letting go of the troubles of the day and feeling more relaxed.

As you read the story, try to keep your voice calm but nevertheless expressive and enthusiastic. The aim is to help your child to enjoy and understand the story, so slow your pace and pause at different points so that she can reflect for a moment, ask questions or make comments. She may like

to suggest voices for the different characters, or predict
what is going to happen next and how the story will end.

The illustrations accompanying each story can serve as
a launching pad for further ideas. Point out details to your
child and ask her to tell you about what she sees. You may
well find that your child's imagination is so fired by these
bedtime stories that the characters and the storylines
influence, either directly or indirectly, her art and craft
activities and make-believe play over the following days and
weeks. If she seems interested, you might like to encourage
her to make up her own fairy stories to tell to you or her
siblings and friends.

The affirmations that conclude each story are there to
encourage a positive, peaceful and calm sense of resolution
for your child. You could discuss them with her, exploring
anything that troubles or confuses her about the story.
Listen carefully to what she has to say, taking note of what
she likes and dislikes about the characters and events, and
provide reassurance and explanations if necessary. As she
drifts quietly to sleep, gently kiss her goodnight and wish
her pleasant dreams.

A Splash
of Fun!

Relax and empty your mind of everyday thoughts. Be still and listen carefully to this story about how fun and mischief bring unexpected smiles.

Term-time at the fairy academy had finished and now it was the holidays. The end-of-term bell rang and all the little fairies flew out across the lake.

"Look at that old lady in the deck chair!" giggled Lenny the wood fairy. "She's always here, sitting by the water. Doesn't she have anything else to do?"

"She must like it here," said Lenny's brother, Larry. "But you wouldn't think so to look at her. She always seems so cross ... a bit like a grumpy old frog!"

"A frog!" chuckled Lenny. "That's funny."

"Her name is Great Aunt Iris," said Wendy the water fairy. "I've heard about her. She used to come to the lake with her nieces and nephews when they were little. And when they were grown up she came with all their children. But now

23

nobody visits her anymore. I expect it's because she's always in a bad mood."

The fairies swooped down to Great Aunt Iris and hovered behind her back, giggling. She didn't notice a thing when Lenny dropped some daisies on to the brim of her big straw hat.

"Has she gone to sleep?" whispered Wendy, clamping her hand over her mouth so that Great Aunt Iris wouldn't hear her laughing.

Great Aunt Iris shifted in her deck chair. Then she took off her hat and flapped it in front of her face. Lenny yelled in fright and all the fairies flew straight up in the air and out of reach.

"It's too hot," grumbled Great Aunt Iris to herself. "I wish it would rain!"

"That was a close one!" said Lenny. "Come on, you two! Let's leave that old grouch alone before she spots us. I'll race you to the island. Last one there is a mouldy toadstool!"

He shot off across the lake. Wendy and Larry chased after him. They didn't give another thought to Great Aunt Iris for the rest of the day.

The friends raced around the island. They played hide-and-seek among the rocks. And, just before it was time to fly home, they played a big game of SPLASH in the lake to cool down.

Next day, Great Aunt Iris was beside the water again, with her big floppy hat pulled down over her face. The fairies hovered above her, listening to the strange old lady talking to herself.

"This awful sun!" she was complaining. "It gets in my eyes. And I can hardly breathe in this heat." A dragonfly streaked past, right under her nose, and she swiped at it with her handkerchief. "Shoo!" she snapped.

"What a misery guts!" exclaimed Larry.

"Imagine shouting at a dragonfly!" said Wendy. "I think they're so beautiful."

"Come on!" said Lenny. "Let's not worry about her. Let's make a camp."

The three friends spent all day long building their camp among the reeds. Finally it was finished.

"And now let's play SPLASH," shouted Lenny. "I need to cool down!" The three fairies jumped into the water and SPLASHED ... right beside Great Aunt Iris!

"What was that?" cried Great Aunt Iris. She jumped up from her chair, looking furious. There were wet patches all over her skirt.

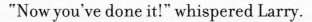

"Now you've done it!" whispered Larry.

Wendy flew forward to apologize. "I'm very sorry!" she said. "We didn't mean to splash you. We were just playing a game to cool down!"

"Goodness gracious!" gasped Great Aunt Iris. "Fairy folk!" As she spoke her crinkled old face broke into an enormous smile.

"Wow! You look happy!" said Larry.

"Not a bit like a grumpy frog," giggled Lenny.

"A frog?!" exclaimed Great Aunt Iris.

"I'm sorry," blushed Wendy. "Fairies are always cheeky, you know!"

But Great Aunt Iris threw back her head and roared with laughter.

"I have been a bit of an old grump," she said. "A frog, eh? Is that what you call me?"

Lenny nodded.

"I'll show you a frog!" With that, Great Aunt Iris tucked up her skirt and leapt into the water.

All afternoon, Great Aunt Iris played SPLASH with the fairies. It was the best game ever!

"I really didn't mean to be grumpy," said Great Aunt Iris as they sat together on the bank to dry. "It used to be my favourite thing to sit here and watch the children splashing each other in the water. We used to have such fun together. But now the children are all grown up and they're too busy with their own lives to visit me. I get so cross sitting here all by myself, with nothing to take my mind off feeling hot."

"From now on we'll come and visit you every day," said Lenny.

"As long as you promise not to be grumpy," said Larry.

"And not to splash us too hard," giggled Wendy, as they all charged back into the water, laughing and shouting, for one last game.

Affirmations

- A few kind words and a friendly smile can go a long way toward cheering someone up.
- Including people in your games always makes them feel happy! Remember this next time you see someone in the playground looking left out.
- When people are bad-tempered, it might just be because they are sad about something in their own life, rather than anything to do with you.

The Get-better Garden

Close your eyes and imagine that you are lying in a garden on a warm day. You can hear all kinds of things moving around you — a beetle crawling up a blade of grass, a bee collecting nectar from a flower. A garden is wonderful place to be.

Listen to this story about a little girl called Laura and the flower elf who helped her to get better when she was ill.

The doctors didn't know what was wrong with Laura. They told her to spend lots of time resting in the fresh air. Laura's house had a beautiful garden, so every day her mother spread a rug and cushions on the grass so that Laura could lie down outside. But even though all the plants around her were growing bigger and stronger, Laura still felt weak. Her mother and father didn't know what to do.

"Give her time," said their old, wise gardener. "She'll become strong again. Plenty of sunshine and lots of healthy food — that's what she needs."

Days passed. Then one morning a doctor told Laura that she would have to go into hospital if she wasn't any better by the end of the week.

That afternoon Laura lay on her rug as usual. She felt very sorry for herself and a big tear rolled down her cheek and trickled into the corner of her mouth.

"Don't cry," said a high, silvery voice. "I'm here to help you grow strong again."

Laura opened her eyes and saw a tiny boy wearing a yellow tunic with a blue kerchief tied around his neck. He had an orange cap and long boots, one red and one purple. A minute trowel and watering can hung from his belt. At first she thought she was dreaming, but even when she blinked the boy was still there.

"I'm real," said the boy, laughing. "I'm a flower elf and my name is Anther. That's also the name for the part of a flower that helps other flowers grow." He looked into Laura's face. He had beautiful eyes – bright green, flecked with gold.

Laura opened her mouth to speak, but Anther held up his hand.

"I'm supposed to be invisible to the likes of you so we have to pretend you can't see me, otherwise my magic won't work." He grinned at her. "Do you understand?"

Laura nodded. For the first time in a long while she felt a shiver of excitement rush through her.

Anther tapped her fingers with his trowel.

"Close your eyes and open your hand," he said. "I'm going to put a magic seed on your palm. When you feel it, squeeze your fingers tight and think about the most beautiful flower you can imagine."

Laura closed her eyes and felt a hard, round seed like a tiny pebble in the palm of her hand. She tried to picture the loveliest flower ever.

Then something extraordinary happened. The seed in her hand began to fizz like a firework!

"Now open your eyes and plant the seed. As you do so, think of yourself," said Anther, his eyes twinkling. "I'll do the rest."

Laura bent down, made a little hole in the earth with her fingers and carefully put in the seed. When she looked up, Anther had gone.

From that moment on, Laura began to get better. When the doctor came, he was so pleased with her progress that he said she wouldn't have to go to hospital after all.

Spring turned to summer and every day Laura lay on her rug in the garden. The seed Anther had given her had grown into a tall, strong plant and every time Laura looked at it, she tried to imagine what it would look like when it blossomed.

One morning, as the sun rose and light crept over the garden, Laura woke up with the strangest feeling. It was as if there were a hundred butterflies inside her. Somehow she just knew that the first flower on her plant had opened.

Laura jumped out of bed and threw back the curtains. The whole garden was covered in thousands of flowers! Reds, purples, oranges, yellows, blues …

Laura ran down the stairs two at a time – the very same stairs that she had been carried down just a few weeks before, because she couldn't manage them alone. But Laura didn't think of that now. All she wanted was to see Anther again and she knew that he would be waiting for her.

Sure enough, the elf was sitting on top of the flower she had planted, a huge grin on his face. He jumped up and held out his arms at the flowers around him.

"You made all these flowers grow!" he cried, leaping up onto Laura's shoulder. "And you did it all on your own because now you're strong and healthy, just like they are."

Then he disappeared. And in that second all the thousands of flowers disappeared with him. All except for one!

Laura looked down at the flower she had planted with Anther. Its petals were all the colours that she had imagined and it was the most beautiful thing that Laura had ever seen.

That morning the doctor came to visit for the last time. Everyone agreed that Laura was well again, even though no one could say exactly what had been wrong with her or why she had got better.

But Laura knew what had cured her, although she never told anyone about it … because it was magic and a secret between her and the flower elf!

Affirmations

- If you are tired or unwell, just going outside to look at the natural world can help you to feel better.
- It is not always easy to trust in your own powers, but believing in yourself keeps you strong and healthy.
- Try to be patient when you are recovering from illness, as it can sometimes take longer than you expect to get better.

The Promise
of Snow

Close your eyes and imagine a winter's day. The air is cold and the sky is heavy with dark clouds. You are longing for it to snow properly, but only rain falls.

Listen to this story about a small fairy who makes a very big promise … perhaps a little too big? Let's see what happened …

Gabby the garden fairy flittered onto the bird table and shivered. It was an icy morning and she was glad that she was wearing her little mittens. Suddenly the door to the house burst open and the twins came running out.

"Still no snow!" sighed Maria, cosy in her bobble hat.

"It's never going to snow!" said Joe. He let go of the sledge he was pulling and kicked at the path grumpily.

Gabby gazed up at the clouds. She, too, wished it would snow. She hated to see the twins so sad.

"I want to build a giant snowman," said Maria.

"And I want to toboggan down the hill," said Joe.

"It will snow tomorrow!" cried Gabby. She flew down from the bird table. "I promise."

"Wow!" cried the twins. "Are you a real fairy?"

"Yes!" Gabby turned a somersault in the frosty air, flapping her wings as if to prove she was real.

"Then it *will* snow tomorrow!" beamed Joe.

"Yes, because a fairy promised it would!" said Maria.

Later that day, Gabby stood in front of the Fairy Queen.

"I am not pleased," said the Queen. She lifted her wand and sparks of white light shot out, dancing like snowflakes.

"You should have seen the children's faces!" said Gabby. "They looked so excited when I promised it would snow."

"But you can't promise it will snow, can you?" chided the Queen. "You have no power over the snow."

Gabby shook her head sadly, her wings drooping.

"I know you only wanted to make the children happy," the Queen said, more kindly. "But you shouldn't make a promise you cannot keep."

"I thought …" said Gabby. "Maybe …" She took a step closer to the Queen and her words came out in a rush. "Your Majesty, could you make it snow?"

"Even I have no power over the weather," said the Queen. "Go back to the twins, and say sorry."

Gabby looked up at the grey clouds floating overhead.

"Maybe it *will* snow tomorrow," she said as she crossed her fingers. "Then my promise will come true all by itself!"

But the next day came and it did not snow.

"I'm sorry!" said Gabby to the twins. "I should never have made that promise. I don't know when it will snow."

"We don't mind!" laughed Joe.

"We met a real fairy!" said Maria. "That's much more exciting than snow!"

A week later it did snow. Gabby played with the twins all day. They flew down the steep hill on the toboggan, and they built a giant snow fairy with huge white wings.

"Will you play with us again tomorrow?" asked Maria.

"Yes!" said Gabby. "And that's a promise I can keep!"

Affirmations

- Your promises are important to other people, so only make promises that you can keep.
- Real friends just want you to be who you are — so there's no need to make up things to impress them.
- Each time of year has its own special weather for you to enjoy, so make the most of each season while it's here.

Molly and the Moonlight Fairy

Relax and empty your mind of everyday thoughts. Be still and listen carefully to this story about a tiny fairy who helped a little girl face up to a big change in her life.

Molly lay tucked up in her little wooden bed in her room right at the top of the house. She was listening to the familiar, comforting sounds of traffic on the road far below. Through the open window she could hear the cars swishing past, the buses trundling down to the bus stop and in the distance the trains rattling over the rails. Molly had fallen asleep listening to these sounds ever since she'd been a baby.

"But now we're moving house, and this is the last time I'll ever sleep in this bedroom," she thought. A lump rose in her throat.

Molly watched as a thin sliver of moonlight danced across the bedroom floor — the tidy bedroom floor! Molly's room had never EVER been this tidy before. But now everything had been packed up in boxes or taken downstairs, ready to be loaded into the removal van in the morning. Her books and toys were stowed away ... the funny cuckoo clock Dad had given her was in her trunk ... even her desk and chair had gone. There was nothing left, apart from her snug little bed and a few favourite soft toys that she couldn't bear to shut up in a box.

"I'll really miss this house," thought Molly. "And I'll miss my bedroom most of all."

She hated the idea of sleeping somewhere new, leaving behind the attic room that she loved so dearly. A tear trickled down her nose.

"Don't cry," said a tiny, tinkling voice.

"Hello!" Molly shouted in surprise and her eyes darted all over the room. There was no sign of the voice's owner.

"I must be dreaming," Molly sighed — and then she gasped. A little silver fairy flew in through the open window, flitted along the path of moonlight and hopped onto the end of her bed. The fairy's pretty dress sparkled like stardust, and her long hair streamed behind her in the night breeze.

"What's the matter, Molly?" asked the fairy, kindly. "You look sad."

"I don't want to move house!" said Molly. "I like it here."

"I know new things can be scary," said the moonlight fairy, her wings fluttering as she spoke, "but I bet you'll love your new house. Just you wait and see!"

"But I want to stay in *this* house!" said Molly, tears rolling down her cheeks. "I don't want anything to change!"

"Let me show you something," said the fairy, flitting back to the windowsill. "Look, Molly, it's a full moon tonight!" The fairy pointed to the big, round disc hanging like a lantern in the sky above the city roofs. "But just watch and wait. Little by little, night by night, the moon will seem to change shape. It won't look round anymore. It will get thinner and thinner."

"Until it looks like a slice of lemon," smiled Molly.

"Exactly," agreed the fairy. "Each day after full moon, as the moon spins around the Earth, the part of the moon that is lit up by the sun gets smaller, and this makes it look like the moon itself is getting smaller."

"And then after a while it starts to gets bigger again," said Molly proudly. She knew a lot about the moon. Her attic window was perfect for watching the way its shape changed in the night sky.

"That's right," said the fairy. "As the moon carries on spinning around the Earth, more and more of it is lit up by the sun, and this makes it look bigger and bigger."

"I know!" said Molly. "I've seen it get bigger, too."

"And, eventually, there will be a full moon again. Just like the one you can see tonight," said the fairy. "Things seem to change, but often the really important things stay just as they always were."

"Like my new house?" asked Molly. She was beginning to understand.

"Right again!" the fairy did a delighted dance across the windowsill. "Your new house will look different. And sound different. Maybe even smell different. But it will still be your home. Your family will still live there with you. Your mum and dad will still tuck you up in your nice wooden bed each night!"

"I think I know what you mean...." said Molly, although she wasn't quite sure.

But before very long, Molly understood completely what the fairy had meant.

Her new room was also high up in an attic. But now, instead of cars and buses and trains, she could hear the call of seagulls and the waves washing up on the shore. Sometimes, she could even hear the hoot of ocean liners out at sea.

But lots of things were the same as they'd always been. Molly hung her funny cuckoo clock on the wall and put her desk and chair beneath the window. And Mum and Dad still read her stories every night and tucked her up in the same little wooden bed.

"And, of course, the moon still shines in on me!" laughed Molly, picking her way through the familiar mess of toys and puzzles on the floor.

She walked over to her window and opened it to let in the little moonlight fairy — just as she always did now, whenever there was a full moon.

Affirmations

- A new situation can seem so scary at first that you can't see anything to like about it, but it will soon become familiar and comfortable.
- The rhythms of nature have lessons for us all — think of the seasons changing and returning again year after year.
- Talking to a fairy friend — or just to one of your ordinary friends — can reassure you when you are afraid.

The Fairy
Trap

Relax and empty your mind of everyday thoughts. Be still and listen carefully to this story about cabbage patch fairies and how a little boy showed his love for wild things.

Toby crept down the garden path, an empty jar tucked snugly under his arm. Grandpa was still asleep.

"You've got to get up early if you want to catch a fairy," giggled Toby to himself.

He could see the glow of the fairy lights now. Tiny shimmering specks, flitting above Grandpa's cabbage patch. Toby had seen the lights the first morning of his visit to Grandpa's house. Since then he had tried every morning to catch a fairy for himself. But they were too fast, twisting and turning through the sky.

"But I WILL catch one today," said Toby under his breath. "It's my last chance."

His mother was coming to collect Toby that very evening, so he had to catch a fairy now if he wanted to take it home

45

and keep it for ever. He crouched down in the long, damp grass at the edge of the cabbage patch and watched the shining specks of golden light dancing around each another.

WHOOSH! A tiny fairy shot past in front of him. Toby held up the jar ... but it was too late. The speck of light was speeding away across the cabbages.

WHEEE! Another fairy whooshed by, this time just above his head, too quick for him to catch.

WHUMP! Something flew into the jar. Toby couldn't believe it. "Got you!" he cried. A tiny fairy had flown straight into his trap!

He pushed the cork into the jar, as tightly as he could. He had made air holes in the cork so that the fairy could breathe. And he'd put cabbage leaves in the bottom in case that is what fairies eat.

Toby ran back up to the cottage and flung open the door.

"What've you got there?" asked Grandpa.

"Oh, nothing." Toby slipped the jar into the deep pocket of his dressing gown. "I just went out looking for ..."

"Butterflies?" asked Grandpa. "Did you catch any?"

"No ... not really," said Toby.

"It's probably best," said Grandpa. "Butterflies nearly always die once you've trapped them, you know."

"Really?" Toby glanced down. He could see the light from the fairy glowing faintly in the pocket of his dressing gown.

"It'll be alright," he thought. "Fairies are magic. They must be stronger than butterflies. I'm sure of that."

"Now," said Grandpa, "who'd like some scrambled eggs?"

As soon as breakfast was over, Toby ran upstairs. He'd already laid out a tray on the bed with a pair of tweezers and the big magnifying glass Grandpa had given him for looking at insects in the garden.

"Here goes," he said, starting to ease out the cork. "Let's have a proper look at you."

WHOOSH! The tiny fairy dashed to the top of the jar.

"Yikes! You're too quick for me!" Toby pushed the cork fully in again. "I'll just have to look at you in the jar. I'm not going to let you out. I'm never going to let you escape."

The light sank down again, drifting slowly toward the cabbage leaves at the bottom of the jar. Toby grabbed the magnifying glass and held it up against the jar.

"Wow!" Close up he could see the fairy in detail. She was no taller than his little finger, but she looked exactly like a real girl ... except, of course, she had shimmering wings.

Her hair was long and fiery red, and she wore a dress made of pieces of cabbage leaf. Her feet were bare and he could even count ten tiny toes.

The fairy put her face right up against the glass. Although she was so small, Toby could make out what she was saying.

"Help! Let me out!" she was crying in her minute voice, big tears rolling down her cheeks.

Toby dropped the magnifying glass. Without hesitation, he flung open the window and uncorked the jar.

"Go!" he said. "Go and be free!"

The speck of light shot away across the garden. Toby watched, hoping he would see the fairy's light fly all the way back to the cabbage patch. But the sunlight was too bright, and the spark was too tiny. Toby soon lost sight of the glow.

"Goodbye!" he called, and he set the jar down on the windowsill. "I'm sorry I scared you."

"Who are you talking to?" came a voice from below.

Toby looked down and saw Grandpa on the path beneath his window.

"No one," said Toby. "I was just ..."

"Gracious!" cried Grandpa. "Just look at that!"

A great ball of light – like the rising sun – flew up out of the cabbage patch. It shimmered in the air for a moment,

glowing golden across the garden. Then
it splintered into a thousand tiny sparkles
and disappeared.

"What was it?" said Grandpa. "It looked like a flash
of lightning. But there's no thunderstorm."

"It looked a bit like fireworks," said Toby.

"But there's no celebration," said Grandpa.

"You never know," smiled Toby. "Perhaps there is."

Toby knew exactly what he had seen. All the fairies had
risen up with joy in a great ball of light, welcoming back
home the fairy that he had trapped.

Toby glanced down at the empty jar. Although he had so
wanted to keep the fairy, he was glad that he had let her go.
He knew that he had done the right thing.

Affirmations

- Be kind to wild creatures and let them remain free, rather than trying to
  keep them for yourself.
- Loving nature is about showing respect for other living things, no matter
  how tiny or strange they are.
- If we love someone, it's important to think about their feelings, not just
  about our own.

Lost in the Fog

Relax and empty your mind of everyday thoughts. Be still and listen carefully to this story about a young bird that needed help when he was lost.

A flock of swallows had gathered on the roof of the barn, huddling together for warmth. The winter wind whipped through the farmyard.

"Brrrr!" said the smallest swallow. He flapped his wings and puffed out his feathers. "Shall we fly about and have a game of chase to try to keep warm?" he asked his friends.

"Oh no!" said an older swallow. "We must save our energy. We'll be flying south for the winter tomorrow."

"Tomorrow?" said the smallest swallow. "Hooray!"

The swallows flew south every year to spend the winter somewhere warm. The smallest swallow had only hatched from his egg that summer so he had never made the journey before. But he had heard all about the exciting trip across the sea, above mountains and over deserts.

"I can't wait to get going!" he said.

First thing the next morning the birds took off.

"This is so exciting!" cried the smallest swallow as he looped the loop.

"Steady!" said a wise old swallow. "You'd better save your energy. We've a long journey ahead of us."

But the smallest swallow did not listen. He darted away to the very front of the flock. "I can keep up with the leaders!" he thought.

"Look at me!" he cried. He ducked and dived and swooped among his friends. "This is so much fun," he called, flying higher than anyone else.

But very soon his wings began to feel weak.

"Are we nearly there yet?" he asked.

"No," said another swallow. "We've still a long way to go."

The smallest swallow flapped his tired wings and tried to keep up. But very soon he was flying at the back of the flock.

"I'm so tired now!" he groaned.

The swallows flew on, through the wind and rain. Suddenly they hit a bank of fog.

"Stick together!" called the swallows at the front. "Fly in a straight line and stay close, so no one gets lost."

The flock disappeared into the deep blanket of fog.

"Wait for me!" shouted the smallest swallow. "I can't see where I'm going."

But the thick fog swallowed up his voice.

"Hello!" he cried. "Can anyone hear me?"

The smallest swallow could only see shadows and strange shapes ahead of him. He had lost sight of his friends.

"Is that you?" he called, swooping down to a big dark shape that he thought might be the flock of swallows.

"Moo!" It was just an old dairy cow.

"Have you seen my friends?" the swallow called.

The cow shook her head. "Get along, little swallow. Fly away," she scolded.

The swallow flew on as the thick fog swirled around him.

"Is that you?" he cried, calling out to some fluttering shapes he saw ahead.

But as he flew closer, he saw that they were not his friends. They were just dry leaves blowing in the wind.

"Help!" he shouted. His wings were so tired now, he could barely keep moving. "I must find my friends. Which way is straight ahead?" he wondered aloud.

"Not this way!" mooed a voice below him. "So don't come and bother me again."

"I'm flying around in circles!" cried the smallest swallow, seeing the grumpy cow beneath him once more. "I'm back where I started."

Feeling very confused, he turned and flew in the opposite direction. His tiny heart was pounding in his chest.

"My friends have gone," he said to himself. "I've no idea which way to fly. I'll be lost for ever in this fog."

"Follow me!" said a tiny voice ahead of him. "I'll lead you back to safety."

"Who are you?" asked the swallow, searching through the greyness to see who had spoken.

But the voice did not reply.

"It was probably just the wind," thought the swallow.

His wings ached but he kept on flying. Ahead of him he saw a light — no bigger than a firefly.

"Wait!" he called. But the light flickered and moved on.

The smallest swallow flapped his wings as hard as he could. He followed the little light on and on through the blanket of fog.

"It's as if the light is guiding me," he thought.

Sure enough, just when he felt he could fly no further, he came out of the fog and into a bright sunny sky. Just ahead of him he could see the flock of swallows, swooping over a cliff and out to sea.

"There you are!" they cried and they turned back so that he could join them.

The smallest swallow told them all about his adventures. "I thought I heard a voice," he said. "But it never spoke to me again."

"It must have been a fog fairy," said the wise old swallow beside him. "It was her light that guided you back to us."

"Thank you kind fairy!" cried the smallest swallow. He hoped that his voice would carry back to her across the sea.

For the rest of the journey, the smallest swallow stuck close to his friends, flying slowly and carefully on and on until, at last, they reached warm and sunny lands.

Affirmations

- Sometimes it is important to save our energy and focus on the one big task that lies ahead.
- When you are doing something for the first time, listen to the advice of people who have done it before.
- When you are trying to do something that seems impossible, just keep going and you will win through in the end.

The Fidget
Fairy

Relax and empty your mind of everyday thoughts. Be still and listen carefully to this story about a little fairy that *couldn't* sit still!

The midday sun was beating down on the fairies' favourite flower meadow. There wasn't a whisper of wind.

"I'm too hot," sighed Fairy Princess Flit. She wriggled around on a buttercup and jiggled her toes. "My wings are tingling, my head is itching and my nose is burning," she groaned. "I wish there was a breeze!"

"Shhhh! Do try to sit still!" said the Fairy Queen. "We're having a very important meeting!"

"Yes," said the King. "There'll be real trouble in the meadow if the wind doesn't blow soon."

Flit flopped down onto her back. She stared up at the bright, blue sky. "Everyone's so grumpy," she whispered to her best friend Twinkle, who was perched on a clover flower beside her. "It's because it's so hot, I suppose."

"They're worried because there's no wind," said Twinkle. "Let's listen."

"Without the wind, this meadow will die!" the King was saying.

Flit sat up. "Why will the meadow die, Papa?"

"Normally, the west wind comes whooshing through this meadow," explained the King. "It scatters all the flower seeds, carrying them far and wide so that new flowers will grow the following year."

"Like the dandelion puffs?" asked Flit, pointing to the big, white, fluffy balls of seeds. "Puff!" She blew on it, wishing she could scatter the seeds across the field like the wind. But her fairy breath wasn't strong enough.

"Your father is right, Flit," said the Queen. "Without the wind the flower seeds won't find somewhere new to grow."

"What we need is a plan," said the King. The grown-ups went back to discussing the problem. Meanwhile Flit lay back and wriggled her legs in the air again.

"I wish this meeting would end. Then Papa could take us to Dragonfly Lake. I'm bored just sitting here," she moaned. She tossed and turned, kicking her feet.

"Sit still, Flit ..." began the King, but then he gasped as tiny, white, feathery seeds filled the air.

"Look! Flit's fidgeting has freed the seeds!" cried Twinkle.

Everyone cheered as Flit wriggled again, sending another puff of dandelion seeds flying into the air.

"Come on!" she cried. "Follow me!"

All afternoon the fairies flew across the meadow shaking the flowers and sprinkling seeds over the ground.

"It's the best game ever," giggled Flit as they chased after each other, trying to be the first to reach the next seed puff.

"The seeds are scattered, ready to grow next spring!" cried the King, when the fairies had shaken every seedhead they could find. "Now let's fly over to Dragonfly Lake. After all that effort, we need a cooling swim!"

Affirmations

- Things that we get into trouble for in one situation might turn out to be helpful in another — but it can be hard to know what is appropriate when!
- Have patience if you want a treat. Once all the work has been done, you can relax and play.
- If you sow seeds now, new life will grow in the future — although you may not know exactly when.

A Pearl
Ring

Close your eyes and imagine that you are at the seaside, walking on the beach. Your bare feet sink into the damp sand. You can feel the sun on your head and hear the sound of seagulls shrieking.

Listen to a story about sea sprite who lived in a rock pool and a boy called Edward who loved to visit his grandmother at the seaside.

One day Edward was playing on the beach with his grandmother. She was walking up and down the beach collecting shells and Edward was turning somersaults. He turned over and over, until he found himself in front of a rock pool.

Edward crouched down and looked into the clear, sparkling water. Tiger-striped fish darted through the strands of seaweed that fluttered on the rocks and a red crab crept over the sand. He noticed a pale seahorse drifting slowly through the shadows.

Then he saw something really amazing! At the bottom of the rock pool a tiny, silver boy was sitting on a stripy shell, blowing bubbles. He waved to Edward and swam up to the surface.

"Don't look so surprised," said the silver boy as he climbed out of the water. He was carrying a pearl ring over his shoulders. He was so small the ring looked as big as a hula-hoop, and the pearl was almost the same size as his head. "I'm a sea sprite," said the tiny boy. "I've lived here for a thousand years, you know."

"I've never seen a sea sprite before," said Edward, blinking his eyes. He still couldn't believe he was looking at one now.

"We don't usually show ourselves. But I particularly wanted to talk to you." The sea sprite held out his hand to Edward, and his touch was as light as a feather. "My name is Kelp," he said, "which is another word for seaweed."

Edward stared even though he knew it was rude.

"Why do you want to talk to me?" he asked.

Kelp shifted the ring from his shoulders.

"A few minutes ago your grandmother dropped her ring in my rock pool," he said.

"Could she see you, too?" asked Edward.

"She saw me before I had time to hide," replied Kelp with a grin. "And she gave me this lovely shell to sit on, which was very kind because all I had before was the sand."

"Granny always makes up stories about fairies and sprites," Edward said laughing. "She thinks they are everywhere."

"She's right," said Kelp. "Although not many other humans know that." He handed Edward the ring. "Please give this back to her. One good turn deserves another."

The next minute the little sea sprite had disappeared among the rocks. And all that was left was a trail of silver bubbles in the water.

Affirmations

- What goes around comes around: if you do something nice, you can expect something nice to happen to you.
- If you believe in magic, magical things may happen.
- A rock pool isn't much to look at from a distance, but it contains some of nature's most wonderful treasures – discover them for yourself next time you go to the seaside.

Sandstorm in the Desert

Close your eyes and imagine that you are lying in a huge tent in the desert. Richly woven carpets cover the ground and the tent is lined with embroidered quilts the colours of jewels. The night is silent and the air is filled with the sweet smell of sandalwood incense.

Listen to this story about a fairy that helped a boy named Abdul who was stranded in the desert during a sandstorm.

Fairies can be found everywhere, and in the deserts of Arabia they are called jinn. The amazing thing about jinn is that they can change their shape into anything they want.

Abdul was travelling on foot with his family, leading their herd of goats to an oasis. It was going to take them many days to get there.

One night, Abdul woke up and saw a shooting star through the open flap of his tent. Shooting stars bring good luck in the desert and Abdul ran outside hoping to see some more.

It was then that Abdul noticed that two of the goats had broken out of their pen and were wandering away over the sand. Abdul didn't think to wake his parents. He grabbed a rope and ran after the goats. But every time Abdul tried to tie the rope around them, they managed to escape.

By the time Abdul caught the two goats, they were halfway up a rocky slope and a long way from the tent. As he started to climb down, he heard a strange roaring noise coming from the other side of the plain. He looked up and his heart stuck in his throat. A huge sandstorm was rolling toward him. Abdul needed to find shelter quickly, but his parents' tent was too far away. Where could he go?

Suddenly a bright orange light, like a flame, appeared in front of him. It moved back and forth among the rocks, almost as if it wanted him to follow, but Abdul kept his distance. His grandmother used to tell him stories about jinn shining in the desert, though he had never believed in them. He wondered what the orange light could be — perhaps something to do with the sandstorm?

The roaring of the storm grew louder and he felt the first prickles of sand in his nose. Abdul saw his father run from the tent and heard the faint cry of his voice. Tears welled up in Abdul's eyes. His parents must have discovered that he

was missing, but there was nothing they could do as the sandstorm was approaching fast.

The flame swooped back and this time it hung in the air right in front of Abdul. He gasped when he saw, in the middle of the flame, a tiny, fat man – a jinni!

"You insult me by ignoring me, you silly boy!" cried the jinni. "Follow me, or you and your goats will never see sunrise again!"

As the sandstorm swallowed up the desert below, the jinni led the way to a cave. Then he vanished into the storm.

For three days Abdul huddled with his goats inside the cave while the sandstorm raged outside. All they had to drink and eat was a trickle of water that ran down the wall of the cave and some green plants that grew in the damp sand.

On the fourth morning the sky was clear and Abdul rushed to the mouth of the cave. But his parents' tent had gone!

Abdul sat down on a rock and howled like a baby.

Below the ledge he was sitting on, a camel coughed and spat. It was such a rude noise, it sounded as if the camel was laughing at him. "Stupid thing!" said Abdul.

The camel made another rude noise, even louder. Then it spoke to Abdul!

"Silly boy!" he said. "Did you think I would leave you here? Hurry up now and climb on my back. I've many others to care for, not just you."

"What about my goats?" asked Abdul in a nervous, squeaky voice.

The camel made another rude noise.

"Don't worry about them. They'll follow when they're ready. They know what's good for them."

Abdul clambered onto the camel's back.

"I'm sorry I called you stupid, and that I ignored you the other day," he said. "I didn't believe in jinn."

"Pah!" spluttered the camel. "You never listen to your grandmother. She can tell you a thing or two about jinn."

It was the middle of the day when Abdul finally saw palm trees and his parents' tent pitched beside the oasis.

The camel dropped down on its knees.

"Think you can find your way from here?" it belched.

Abdul stood up and shook the sand out of his tunic.

"Yes, I think so," said Abdul. "And thank you for helping me. I'll never forget it."

"You're a silly boy, but you'll learn," the camel grunted, though he sounded pleased.

Then, in front of Abdul's very eyes, the camel turned into a vulture and flapped up and away into the sky. The boy watched as the vulture became a faraway speck and finally disappeared. Then he ran as fast as he could to his parents' tent.

Many years later Abdul told this story to his own grandchildren. He described the feast his parents held to celebrate his safe return and how at the end of the evening his grandmother took him aside.

"You were a lucky boy," she said sternly. "From this day on you must always be kind to any camels you meet. You can never be sure that they won't be your jinni!"

Affirmations

- Nature is full of surprises, some of them dangerous. Be aware of your surroundings and always treat the natural world with respect.
- Help comes from the most unlikely sources, even from people whom you might have thought strange or unfriendly. Accept it thankfully.
- Have faith in the kindness of other people and they will be more likely to help you.

Mia on
Mud Duty

Relax and empty your mind of everyday thoughts. Be still and listen carefully to this story about a fairy who makes a friend and learns to be proud of her work.

"The Fairy Queen is coming to visit our school's garden," said Miss Greenwings, the fairy teacher. "She is going to give a gold medal to the fairy who grows the best flowers."

"How exciting!" cried all the young fairies.

"I'd better make sure my foxgloves are perfect for her visit," said Gloria. Away she flew in her pink petal dress.

"I'd better see to my daisies," said a little fairy called Hannah. And away she flew in her yellow petal dress.

Fairies dressed in petals of every colour flew around the garden. "Hurry!" they cried. "We've so much to do."

No one had more work than Mia. She was on mud duty. Mia's dress was not made of petals. She wore an apron made from a piece of old garden sack, and rubber boots so that she could squelch around in the mud.

"You'd better get busy," said Miss Greenwings. "You have the biggest job of all."

It was Mia's job to keep the garden soil in good condition. She had to water it. And weed it. And rake away the stones so that the flowers could grow tall.

"I wish I could look after a pretty flower instead of the boring old mud," said Mia. "The Queen will never notice my work."

Miss Greenwings smiled and patted Mia's head.

"I know being on mud duty is not very glamorous or showy. But I also know how hard you work. We have the best soil of all the gardens in this town. That is down to your hard work, Mia. I am very proud of you, my dear ... very proud indeed!"

"Thanks," sniffed Mia. She picked up her tiny watering can and flew away. But when she reached the garden tap, she sat down and burst into tears.

"What's the matter?" said a voice from above.

Mia looked up to see a boy standing beside her. He had bright blue eyes and a big friendly smile.

"My name is Josh," he said. "Why are you crying?"

"I'm on mud duty," sobbed Mia. She told Josh about the Queen's visit and how she had no hope of winning the prize.

"I know just how you feel," said Josh. "We did a play at school and a famous film actor came to see it. I wanted to be the Roman Emperor. That was the main part, you see."

"And were you?" asked Mia, flying up onto Josh's outstretched hand.

Josh shook his head. "Nope! I wasn't even a spear-carrier. My teacher put me in charge of the lights. I had to sit high above the stage and no one could see me."

"Poor you!" said Mia.

"That's what I felt ... at first," said Josh. "My teacher told me that lighting was one of the most important jobs, but I thought he was just saying that to be kind."

"Miss Greenwings is just being kind, too," Mia agreed.

"But I changed my mind," said Josh. "On the night of the show there was a power cut. It only lasted about half a minute, but without my lights no one could see anything. When the lights came back up, everyone cheered and clapped. After that, I realized how important my lights were. And when the play was over, the actor made a speech and gave me a special mention!"

"How exciting!" said Mia.

"And your job is just as important as mine was," said Josh. "Without good soil, the flowers will not grow."

"You're right!" cried Mia. "I'd better get on with my work. I've a lot to do before the Queen visits."

All that week Mia tended the soil. By the time the Queen came, there was not a weed or a rock in sight. The flowers stood tall and strong in the perfect, moist earth.

"These are the finest flowers I have ever seen," said the Queen. "The foxglove petals feel like velvet."

"Perhaps I'm going to win the medal," whispered Gloria. She blushed as pink as the petals of her dress.

"And the daisies are such a bright yellow and white," said the Queen.

"Or perhaps I might win," whispered Hannah, crossing her fingers.

"I said I would give a prize for the best flowers," announced the Queen. "But all these flowers are the best of their type that I have ever seen."

She paused and smiled. "Flowers this good can only have come from one thing – great soil!"

And she handed Mia the medal.

"Often it is the jobs no one notices that make the most difference," said the Queen. "Mia, if you had not worked so hard in the mud, the flowers would have shrivelled up and died. Congratulations on a job well done."

74

Mia curtseyed.

"Do come to tea with me at the palace tomorrow," said the Queen. "I'd love you to give me some tips so that I can make the flowers in my garden bloom as beautifully as these."

"Thank you!" smiled Mia. "I'd like that."

As soon as the Queen had gone, Mia flew away to find Josh. She told him how she had won the prize and about her invitation to the palace for tea.

"I'm going to wear a dress made out of all the different petals in the garden," she said.

"Like a rainbow?" asked Josh.

"Exactly," said Mia "But I'll still wear my old boots in case the Queen wants to squelch in the mud!"

Affirmations

- Sometimes the jobs behind the scenes are the most important of all, the ones that everything else depends on.
- If you're part of a team, you can achieve results that you would never have managed on your own — and have a lot of fun, too!
- Everything in nature has a role to play in the cycle of life — think of how dead plants decay and nourish the earth from which new plants grow.

A Light
in the Dark

Close your eyes and imagine that you are sitting inside a yellow flower growing on a cactus plant in the desert. Silky petals are all around you and pollen sticks to your fingers like gold dust.

Listen to this story about a desert spirit called Shine, and how she helped a cowboy named Roy and his horse, Nugget, when they got into trouble in the desert.

Shine lived in a cactus flower that only came out at night. When she climbed out to look at the stars, her wings twinkled in the moonlight and she shone in the dark like a silver lamp.

The story begins when Roy decided to visit his mother, who lived next to a river in a canyon two days' ride from Roy's home. Before he reached the river, Roy would have to cross a vast desert with no streams, no food and no shelter from the sun. He knew that he would have to camp overnight in the desert, so he loaded up Nugget with

saddlebags full of food and water, and a warm blanket — deserts are very cold at night. As Roy hadn't seen his mother for a long time, he also packed lots of presents for her. Just after dawn he set off, wearing his cowboy hat to protect him from the blazing sun.

The desert stretched as far as Roy could see, covered with boulders, prickly bushes and cactus plants. There was no sign of water or any other living being. It would be a long ride, but Roy wasn't worried. He had made the journey many times before.

They rode for hours and it began to get dark. Roy was wondering how long it would take to reach the hidden gully where he always camped when suddenly Nugget stumbled and Roy fell to the ground.

"Steady there, girl!" he said, patting Nugget. He tried to climb back on but Nugget whinnied in pain and pulled away, limping. "You twisted your fetlock, girl?" Roy asked. (The fetlock is like an ankle on a person and twisting it is a very serious injury for a horse.) "Don't worry. We'll get it looked at as soon as we can tomorrow."

Roy heaved all the bags onto his back and set off, leading Nugget and looking for the gully. He whispered reassuring

words to the horse, but he was worried.
They were only halfway through the journey.

"I'll just have to leave Ma's presents here," he said,
hiding all but one of the bags behind a boulder. Roy knew
that he couldn't carry them by himself. He and Nugget had
gone too far to turn back and there was no one to help them
in the desert — their only option was to go on.

The gully was nowhere to be seen and now it was properly
dark. Roy knew only too well that the desert is a dangerous
place at night and that somehow they had to find
somewhere safe to shelter.

As he looked around at the dark outlines of the cactus
plants against the moonlit sky, Roy remembered a story
he'd once heard from a white-haired cowboy. One time
when the cowboy was lost in the desert, a spirit had
appeared from inside a cactus flower and rescued him!
"Strong as an ox, it was," the old timer had said.

"What hogwash," Roy muttered to himself. "He must
have been crazed by the sun."

At that moment Nugget whinnied and tugged at her reins.

"Come on, girl," said Roy, gently trying to coax her
forward. "We've got to keep moving."

But Nugget snorted and shook her head.

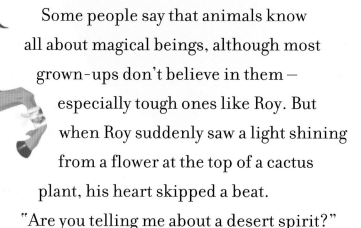

Some people say that animals know all about magical beings, although most grown-ups don't believe in them — especially tough ones like Roy. But when Roy suddenly saw a light shining from a flower at the top of a cactus plant, his heart skipped a beat.

"Are you telling me about a desert spirit?" he asked Nugget as he rubbed her nose.

Instead of responding, Nugget began to tremble. Her fetlock was hurting so much that she just lay down on the sand and refused to get up. It was if time had stopped still. Coyotes barked and an owl screeched from the bushes.

Roy took a deep breath and made himself walk over to the cactus plant. Shine was expecting him, and when the little cactus spirit saw his worried face, she smiled and climbed out of the petals. Roy had never seen anything like her before, but he knew a miracle when he saw one — and a miracle was what they needed.

"Please help us," he whispered.

Shine smiled again and nodded her head once. As she flitted through the air, the light from her wings flowed under Nugget's body like liquid silver.

Roy's mother still tells the story of how she dreamed she saw Roy and Nugget carried across the night sky on two huge silver wings, and how she was woken by the sound of Roy banging on the door. She put them both straight to bed – Roy in his old bedroom and Nugget in the stables with a blanket and plenty of fresh straw.

The next morning, Roy woke up bright and early, his head still full of light from the desert spirit's eyes. He ran over to the stable to see Nugget.

When she heard him coming, Nugget whinnied and snorted. Her fetlock was completely better and she was standing up alert and happy.

Roy didn't know what to think. But from that day on, one more cowboy believed in magic!

Affirmations

- Things rarely turn out exactly as you planned them – be prepared and look for the adventure in every unexpected event!
- Think positively. Even problems that at first seem impossible to overcome have a solution.
- Even an apparently barren landscape like the desert contains secret life and wonderful beauty.

Flying High

Relax and empty your mind of everyday thoughts. Be still and listen carefully to this story about a fairy who showed great courage in order to make a little boy happy.

There was a strong wind blowing across the village green.

"A good wind," said the beech tree fairy.

"A great wind!" said the holly tree fairy.

"Let's play chase-around-the-treetops!" shouted the yew tree fairy.

"Oh dear!" thought the little ivy fairy. "I hope they don't want me to play, too."

But sure enough Beech called out, "Come on, Ivy! The wind is perfect for a game of chase-around-the-treetops."

"It'll be brilliant," said Holly. "We'll fly higher than the church steeple. We'll be able to see the whole village from up there."

"Yippee!" whooped Yew. "Being blown about in the wind is going to be so much fun!"

But Ivy shook her head. "I … um …
I need to tidy my ivy today," she murmured.

"Suit yourself!" said Beech.

"That's a pity!" said Holly.

"Join us later if you want to," added Yew.

"Yes, I might just do that," Ivy replied. But she knew that she would not join them. It was not that she did not like the other fairies. They were her best friends. And it was not that she didn't want to play games.

The fact of the matter was … Ivy was afraid of heights. She did not want to fly so high, especially in this strong wind. Even the thought of it made her tiny tummy flip over with nerves.

Ivy watched while her friends were tossed from side to side, shrieking and giggling as the wind whipped through their wings. Up and up they flew, until they were tiny dots spinning around the steeple. Ivy shivered at the thought.

"It's lonely down here on my own," she said to herself. "But I'm glad I don't have to fly so high."

She flitted over to the market square, where a little boy was trying to fly his kite. Ivy watched him tug at the string.

"There's so much wind, why won't you fly?" he moaned. But the kite just fluttered across the ground.

The boy rolled up the string, picked up the kite and ran across the square. Then he let the kite go. This time the wind caught it. Up it went for a brief moment. Then ... FLOP! Down it fell again.

"Oh, why won't it work?" the boy cried, scuffing his shoes on the ground. He picked up the kite again.

As the little boy came closer, Ivy peeped out from her hiding spot and saw that his eyes were filled with tears of frustration and anger.

"If only he could get the kite higher into the air," she thought. "Then the wind would take it. If only someone could give the kite a bit of a lift ..."

She looked up into the sky for her friends.

"Beech," she called. "Holly, Yew, come quickly! A boy down here needs some help."

But her friends were flying too high to hear. The strong wind carried Ivy's voice away.

The little boy wiped his tears on his sleeve and tried again to make the kite fly.

Bump! Bump! Bump! The kite just bounced along the ground. Ivy knew what she had to do. Before she had a chance to think about it too much, she flew across the square. She was so tiny that the little boy did not see her.

As the kite bumped along, Ivy grabbed its edge and carried it with her. She flew up into the sky.

WHOOSH! As soon as they were high enough, the wind took hold of the kite and carried it upward.

"Yikes!" cried Ivy, holding on tight to the kite.

"Wow!" said the boy far below her. He ran faster and faster, a smile spreading across his face as the kite danced in the wind.

Still clinging to the kite, Ivy was above the treetops now, whizzing past the church steeple. She could see the whole village spread out beneath her – the playground, the streets, the school and the market square.

"Whoopee!" she cried. "Now I'm up here, I don't feel scared at all!"

"That looks like fun!" said a voice beside her, and Beech caught hold of the kite too.

"Brilliant!" yelled Holly.

"Even better than playing chase-around-the-treetops," cried Yew. He grabbed onto the kite as well.

The fairy friends flew on the kite for hours. Every time it fell back to the ground, they helped it into the air once more.

The little boy had no idea that the four tiny

fairies were there. He never guessed why his kite had started flying so well. But he had a brilliant afternoon playing with the wind.

"That really was fun!" said Ivy, when the boy had taken the kite back home at last.

"I loved being up high in the sky," said Holly.

"The wind is still so strong. I wish we could carry on playing," sighed Yew.

"We can't play with the kite anymore," said Ivy. "But who's for a game of chase-around-the-treetops?"

Without waiting for an answer, she shot up into the air – high, high, high above the church steeple.

"Wait!" cried her three friends, and they chased after her, giggling with delight.

Affirmations

- Seeing someone who needs your help can inspire you to be brave even though you feel afraid.
- You don't always have to join in or follow others. It's OK not to do something that your friends are doing, if you don't want to.
- Making up your own games can be fun. And before long, everyone may want to join in!

The Tractor Fairy

Close your eyes and imagine that you are sitting in the long grass at the edge of a field that has just been ploughed. The ground ripples ahead of you like a sea with its waves made out of earth.

Think about what it might be like to drive the tractor that ploughed those long smooth furrows – hands steady on the wheel, turning the corner at each end, and driving up and down, up and down, in the straightest of lines. It would be hard to do, but you would feel so proud of yourself when you had finished!

This is the story of a farmer's son called Evan. As a little boy, Evan had loved playing with tractors. When he was older he learned to drive, and from that day on, he dreamed of the day when he could win the ploughing competition that was held every year at the Farmers' Show.

For Evan there was more to winning the ploughing competition than simply being the

best at ploughing the straightest furrow. Each
year, the winner had his name engraved on a big
silver cup. And Evan wanted *his* name to be on that cup,
just like his father's and grandfather's before him.

Spring arrived and once again it was time for the
Farmers' Show. All the local farmers, young and old, were
there. A grey-haired farmer wearing his best wool suit
tapped Evan on the shoulder.

"You tryin' to win the ploughing competition this year,
boy?" he asked.

Evan nodded. He felt uncomfortable in the stiff red
overalls he'd put on to look smart for the competition,
and wished he was wearing the patched dungarees he
usually pulled on every morning.

"Goin' for the cup, same as yer dad and yer granddad?"
asked the old man.

Evan felt his cheeks growing hot and without saying
anything he nodded again.

The old man smiled. "Good luck, boy," he said.

Two hours later, Evan shook hands with the competition
judges and climbed up into the cab of the old blue tractor
that belonged to his father and had once been his
grandfather's. It was looking a bit battered now,

but his dad said that it still ploughed a good line. Evan settled himself in the seat, turned the key and reached down to release the handbrake.

But then something terrible happened! Evan's glasses slipped off his face and smashed on the metal floor. When he looked up again, Evan couldn't even make out the faces of the spectators outside the tractor. Without his glasses, ploughing in straight lines would be impossible!

Evan felt his stomach turn over. What on earth was he going to do? He knew that he would never forgive himself if he just climbed down from the tractor and gave up.

"Now then, Master Evan," said a squeaky voice. "Don't you worry about nuffin'."

Evan thought his eyes would pop out of his head. Sitting right in front of his nose on the steering wheel was a tiny figure with a greasy face, wearing a pair of dirty dungarees and a flat cap.

"Don't stare so, Master Evan," said the little creature. "Or them eyes of yours will come right out of their sockets."

"Who are you?" gasped Evan.

"I'm the fairy for this old tractor," came the reply.

"Henry, I's called."

Evan stared even harder.

"Do all tractors have fairies?" he whispered.

"Old ones do," replied Henry. He patted the wheel. "They needs lookin' after just like old people, see."

A hooter sounded behind them. They had one minute to get themselves into position at the bottom of the field!

"Come on," cried Henry. "You and me's goin' to win this competition!"

"That's just not possible," said Evan. "I can barely see what's in front of me, let alone drive in straight lines."

"Course it's possible!" yelled the fairy. "Come on!"

Henry jumped onto Evan's shoulder and tugged his ears. First Evan's right ear and then his left. "We do it like this. You drives, I steers."

"This is crazy!" said Evan, but he turned the key in the ignition and let the tractor roll down to the starting point. Screams and laughs came from the crowd outside.

"Watch out!" shouted Henry, tugging violently on Evan's right ear. "You don't want to run anyone over before you've even started."

People still talk of the day when Evan won his first ploughing competition. They say it was a miracle because when Evan was halfway up the field the sky turned black as night and rain began pouring down as heavily as a waterfall. It was hard enough to make out the fingers on the ends of your hands, they say, let alone drive a tractor in the smoothest, straightest lines that anyone had ever seen!

Evan never saw the tractor fairy again, but he always remembered the fairy's kindness. And years later, when he took over the farm, whenever the days grew colder he would always make sure to shelter the blue tractor in a shed at night, and cover the old machine with a blanket to keep it warm and snug.

Affirmations

- Don't feel bad if something happens that's not your fault. We all experience bad luck sometimes.
- A well-made object is something to treasure through the years – new is not necessarily best.
- Kindness doesn't require money or any special ability and is a gift that we all can give every day.

Nest in the Sky

Close your eyes and imagine that you are curled up in a huge, cosy nest made of dry sticks and lined with soft feathers. The nest is high up in a tree in a pine forest. Over the edge of the nest, you can see a mountain peak covered with snow. There are hundreds of thousands of trees in these mountains and in each one of them a tree spirit has made her home.

This story is all about two eagle chicks who got into trouble, and the tree spirit who helped them. The spirit was called Cedar, and the eagle chicks were known as Wriggle and Scratch, because that's what they did when their parents were away hunting.

The story begins when Wriggle and Scratch were almost three months old. They had lots of feathers and could flap their wings about, but they still hadn't learnt how to fly. One morning their parents went off to find food and left them on their own.

"Bet I learn to fly way before you," squawked Wriggle, wriggling about among the sticks and feathers.

"Bet you don't," replied Scratch, scratching his sharp toes along the edge of the nest. "I came out of my egg before you."

"So what?" squawked Wriggle.

"So … I'm older than you," crowed Scratch. He stood up and waggled his wings. "That means I'm stronger than you … and braver than you!"

Wriggle stood up and waggled his wings, too.

"No, it doesn't," he squawked.

"Yes, it does!" insisted Scratch.

And before they knew it, they were jumping about in the nest and flapping their wings at each other. They were making such a noise, they didn't hear the crack! crack! of dry sticks.

Suddenly the bottom fell off the nest!

Wriggle and Scratch had just enough time to grab onto the side of the nest with their talons. A split second later they were hanging upside down looking all the way down to the ground!

Cedar the tree spirit had been watching the two eagle chicks from the moment they hatched out of their eggs in the nest right at the top of her tree. She had lived in that particular tree ever since it had grown strong enough to stand up against the wind, and before that she had lived in hundreds of other trees on the mountain. She was a very ancient spirit.

Even though Cedar knew everything that there was to know about baby eagles and their nests, she firmly believed that spirits should not use their magical powers to interfere in the natural world unless help was desperately needed. She knew that it is always better for young birds and animals to learn how to look after themselves.

But when Cedar saw Wriggle and Scratch hanging upside down, and realized that more and more sticks were falling off the nest, she immediately flew over to them. She could see that the two eagle chicks were frozen with terror, clinging to the ruined nest, too scared to try to help themselves.

"Don't be frightened," said Cedar, using magic to speak to Wriggle and Scratch in

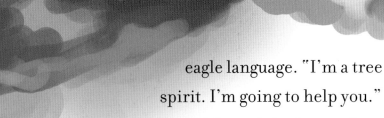

eagle language. "I'm a tree spirit. I'm going to help you."

Wriggle and Scratch had never heard of tree spirits before. They were so surprised that the strange green and gold thing could speak like they did, they almost let go of the nest!

"Hold on tight!" ordered Cedar. She stared into the bulging eyes of the two terrified chicks. "There's only one thing to do!"

"What?!" squawked Wriggle and Scratch at the same time.

"FLY," cried Cedar. She flapped her green wings. "Do what I do! Follow me!"

At that moment, the nest collapsed and the eagle chicks fell out.

"FLY!" cried Cedar again. "Come on! Flap your wings! Be brave!"

"Help!" squawked Wriggle and Scratch as they plummeted toward the ground. They frantically flapped their wings. The two chicks saw flashes of green and gold all around, and then suddenly they felt their wings lifting them through the air.

A moment later they landed safely on a branch in the next tree.

"We did it!" squawked Wriggle.

"We can fly!" crowed Scratch.

Cedar pointed through the branches to where two huge pairs of eagle wings were flapping in the sky, coming toward them. Then she turned to the chicks and grinned.

Without a squawk, Wriggle and Scratch took off from the branch and soared high into the air to meet their parents. They looped the loop and rode the air currents.

It felt amazing. With just a little encouragement from a tree spirit, they had learned to fly!

Affirmations

- If someone is encouraging us, we often find we can suddenly do something that we couldn't do before.
- Always try to build up your friends' confidence when they are attempting something new or difficult.
- If you set your sights high, you'll be able to achieve things that you might not have thought possible.

The Sea Sprite

Close your eyes and imagine that you are lying by the sea. The sun is warm on your face and you can hear the sound of waves splashing along the shore.

This is a story about a sea sprite who was always on the lookout for someone who needed help.

One day two boys came with their mother and grandfather to a saltwater swimming pool on the beach. The huge rock pool was almost like the sea because there were lots of tiny animals and seaweed in the water, but swimming there was safer than in the open sea. Everyone spread out their towels and changed into their bathing suits. All except Grandpa, who lay down on a sun lounger and put his hat over his face.

"Can we go swimming, Mum?" asked the older boy. His name was Alex and he loved to play in the water.

"Of course you can," said their

mother. She turned to her younger son, who was staring unhappily at his feet. "Do you want to come, Tim?"

Tim shook his head.

"I'd rather read a book," he said.

Alex pulled a face.

"Tim's afraid of the water! Tim's afraid of the water!" he sang in a sing-song voice.

"Alex!" said his mother firmly. "Don't be mean. Tim can sit here if he wants to. Grandpa will stay with him." She kissed Tim quickly and jumped into the huge pool with Alex.

Tim watched his brother and mother splashing in the sparkling water and felt bad. The truth was that even though he had taken some swimming lessons, as soon as the water came above his knees he felt so frightened that he didn't want to go in any further.

When Tim was little it hadn't mattered too much, but now everyone in his class at school really loved the water, but he dreaded it. Tim sat beside his grandfather and watched the frilly edges of the waves ripple along the sides of the rock pool and wondered if he would ever like swimming.

At that moment, something extraordinary
happened. More and more bubbles were coming
up to the water's surface, and they seemed
to be forming words ... BE BRAVE ... COME
TO ME. Tim turned to tell his grandfather
what he had seen, but when he looked back to check
that he hadn't imagined it, the words had disappeared.

A flash of light moved back and forth over the water.
Tim thought it might be a fish, but as he stared at it, he had
the strangest feeling. It was as if he was being gently drawn
toward the water.

"I'm going to stand on the steps," he said. The next
minute he was up to his knees in water.

The flash of light hovered in front of him. Tim saw a
tiny silver girl with a horn slung over her shoulder!

"Wow!" said Tim, taking one step, and then another,
toward her.

"My name is Marina," said the girl. "I'm a sea sprite and
I'm here to show you that swimming is the most wonderful
thing there is."

"I'm sure it is," Tim said, smiling sadly. "The problem
is I'm scared."

"Are you scared now?" twinkled Marina.

At that moment, Tim realized two things. He wasn't afraid and his feet were barely touching the bottom!

Tim turned around and saw his grandfather sitting up on the sun lounger, watching him. He was waving and there was a big grin on his face!

"I taught your grandfather how to swim when he was the same age as you," laughed Marina.

Tim couldn't believe his ears! But before he had time to say a single word, Marina dipped her horn in the water and a stream of bubbles made a ring around Tim's middle and under his arms! The next moment he was floating and then suddenly he was kicking his feet and moving his arms! And he loved it.

Later, Tim was sitting by the side of the pool, talking to his grandfather.

"I was afraid of water when I was a little boy," said his grandfather. "Then one day my grandfather brought me here. Of course, it was a beach in those days but I saw the words in the water and the sea sprite appeared in front of me."

Tim's eyes opened wide.

"But that was years and years ago!" he exclaimed.

"Sea sprites have been with us since the beginning of time," his grandfather chuckled.

Tim pulled a face and broke into a huge smile.

"What are you thinking?" asked his grandfather.

"Alex is in for a big surprise!" replied Tim. He punched the air and let out a whoop of delight. Then they both burst out laughing.

Afterwards, Tim could never remember the exact moment when his fear vanished. He just knew that swimming was the most thrilling feeling in the world!

Affirmations

- Be open to new experiences. People often grow to love doing things that they disliked at first.
- Remember that everything happens in its own time. It doesn't matter that some people learn to do things more quickly than others.
- Grandparents are great for sharing your troubles with — they've experienced a lot over the years and can offer good advice.

The Sunflower Race

Relax and empty your mind of everyday thoughts. Be still and listen carefully to this story about a fairy who learned to share with her friends.

It was a beautiful summer's day. Six fairies flew high above the meadow.

"Look at all the sunflowers!" cried Bobby. "They are so bright in the sunshine!"

The fairies agreed. There were sunflowers everywhere, their golden petals reaching for the midday sun. But one sunflower had grown bigger and stronger than the others.

"Race you there!" said Edward.

Angelica had already flown away. Although she was the youngest, she was also the fastest and she knew that she could easily beat her friends in any race.

"The winner is Queen of the Sunflowers!" she cried, leaving the others far behind. Try as they might, the rest of the fairies couldn't catch up.

"You can't rule flowers," panted Emily, who was not very good at flying fast.

"That's right," agreed Bobby, also out of breath as he flapped his wings as quickly as he could. He was feeling cross that a girl fairy was beating him.

"Ha! I am Queen of the Sunflowers!" Angelica cried as she landed on a golden petal. "This one is my castle. None of you can come up here now."

"I wouldn't want to be up there with you anyway!" snapped Bobby. The rest of the sunflowers were too small for all the fairies to sit on together, so they chose a tall, sturdy thistle instead.

"But the sunflower is so pretty. Please let us share it," begged Helena.

"No!" said Angelica. "I won't share it! I want the sunflower all to myself!" And she peered down at her five friends who were crowded onto the fluffy, purple thistle-heads below.

"Suit yourself, Queen Bossy-Wings!" jeered Bobby.

"Watch out!" cried Emily and there were squeals of laughter as Graham wriggled to get comfortable and nearly knocked her off. Everyone jostled and pushed and giggled as they tried to keep their space on the thistle-heads.

"Ouch! I got a prickle in my bottom!" gasped Edward and everyone burst out laughing.

High above them, Angelica sat alone and nibbled a sunflower seed.

"I've got food up here!" she boasted. "You can't eat thistles can you?"

"Can I have a seed?" begged Helena. "I'm starving.

"Me too," said Edward, "I haven't eaten a thing since breakfast."

"And me," pleaded Graham, "Please, Angelica."

"No!" said Angelica, frowning. And she ate two more seeds herself.

The fairies thought that she was being mean and selfish.

"Never mind, I'll find us something to eat," said Graham.

He flew down and plucked a few dandelion leaves from the hedgerow at the edge of the field. They were as much as his fairy arms could carry and he arrived back on the thistle looking pink with all the effort.

"We can all share this," he said.

"This is just like a picnic!" smiled Emily as

they passed the delicious dandelion leaves around, taking little nibbles.

Angelica looked down at the other fairies. It did look fun — all of them squashed together, sharing their snack on top of the thistle. She had been so pleased to win the race and take the sunflower castle for herself … but she longed to join in with her friends.

Now they were playing windy whispers, huddled together in a circle.

"Can I play?" Angelica asked.

"No!" snapped Bobby. "You wanted to be Queen of the Sunflowers, so you can stay up there on your own."

"That's not kind!" said Graham. "Angelica can join us if she wants to."

"But there's no room on the thistle," said Emily, trying to budge up.

"If we let you on, the stalk might snap," said Edward, looking worried.

Angelica glanced at her big empty sunflower. "Then come up here," she said. "I'm sorry I was nasty. There's plenty of room for all of us."

"Will you share the seeds, too?" asked Bobby.

"Of course!" smiled Angelica.

All afternoon, the six friends played windy whispers and danced ring-around-the-sun. They ate their fill of seeds and Bobby impressed everyone by juggling with the seed cases.

"This is much more fun that being on my own," laughed Angelica.

"And much more fun than being pricked on the bottom!" giggled Edward.

Everyone collapsed in fits of laughter.

Affirmations

- Sharing is good for friendships — and wild things like flowers are for everyone to share.
- You can be proud of yourself if you are good at something, without showing off or taking advantage of your friends.
- Be nice to your friends when you have beaten them in a game. If you are mean, they won't want to play anymore.

The Waterfall Fairy

Close your eyes and imagine that you are lying in thick, green grass above a mountain pool. A waterfall is spilling over the rocks in front of you and tiny sparkling droplets fly like silver balls in the air. Sometimes the spray tickles your face and when you laugh, your voice is lost in the sound of splashing water.

This is a story about a fairy named Cera, who lived behind a waterfall in the mountains, and who once helped a young shepherd boy called Claus learn how to look after his sheep.

The only people who ever came to Cera's waterfall were shepherds bringing their flocks to graze on the mountainside during the summer months. Cera had seen many shepherds come and go, because she had lived behind the waterfall for hundreds of years. The shepherds first came to the waterfall as children, accompanied by their parents or older brothers and sisters. Later, when they had

113

learned how to care for the sheep, they would start coming on their own. Cera was fond of the shepherds she had watched grow up.

It was the first time that Claus had been trusted to take his family's flock of sheep up to the summer pasture by himself. He was a gentle boy who loved, more than anything else, to sit outside and daydream while he played his pan pipe. His father was always telling him off for not listening.

"Listen to me, Claus," said his father, firmly. "This is very important. You must remember to take the sheep to drink water every day. Up in the summer pasture there's only one place to go for water … and that's the pool below the waterfall."

But Claus wasn't listening when his father told him how to get to the pool. He was too busy thinking up a new tune for his pipe.

"Will you remember the directions?" asked his father.

"Don't worry," said Claus. "I'll be fine." He didn't want his father to be cross with him for not listening, so he pretended that he knew the way to the pool.

"Mountains are full of streams," he thought. "How hard can it be to find water?"

It was a long climb up to the shepherd's hut on the mountainside and by the time Claus arrived, the sheep were weary and Claus was tired, too. He sat down in front of the hut and fell asleep.

When he woke up it was already dark, so he couldn't even try to find the path to the pool where the sheep were supposed to drink. But Claus was lucky – it had rained the night before, so the sheep were able to drink all that they needed from puddles on the ground.

The next morning the sun came out and there wasn't a cloud in the sky. All day long the sheep wandered about nibbling the grass, while Claus basked in the sunshine, playing his pan pipe and keeping an eye on the flock. But when the sun began to set, the sheep clustered around the shepherd's hut and started bleating.

Claus knew the sheep were thirsty but he couldn't remember how to get to the pool and he hadn't seen a single stream all the time he'd been up on the mountainside. He had no idea what to do. So he did what he always did when he needed help. He played a tune on his pipe. This one made splashy-splashy sounds and Claus hoped that the way to the pool might just appear in his head.

As I said, Claus was a dreamy sort of boy and although he was kind and loved his flock, he wasn't really a shepherd by nature at all.

Luckily the mountains are full of magic. From behind her waterfall, Cera heard the splashy-splashy sounds and wondered who could be playing a pipe.

"Surely it can't be shepherds," she said to herself. "They would have brought the sheep to the pool much earlier in the day."

Then Cera heard another noise. It was sound of sheep bleating unhappily, asking for water. Now she understood that the piper must be a shepherd calling for help.

That night Cera waited until the moon had risen. Then she bent down and drew a picture in a puddle of water that had splashed onto the rock from the waterfall. Her finger traced an outline of the route from the shepherd's hut to the pool. As she drew, the puddle glazed over and, little by little, a map appeared.

Inside the shepherd's hut Claus rolled over and began to have the most extraordinary dream. In his mind he saw a beautiful girl bending over a puddle, running her fingers through the water in different directions.

He knew that she was drawing a map. A second later, Claus woke up and lit a candle. While the image of the map was still clear in his mind, he scratched it in the earth floor of the hut with a stick.

Before dawn the next day, Claus called together his sheep and took them straight to the track that led to the pool at the bottom of the waterfall. As the sun rose, the grateful animals gathered around the pool and drank their fill.

Claus watched the golden light sparkle on the tumbling waterfall. Suddenly, he noticed a shimmering shape on a rock ledge – a fairy! He picked up his pipe and put it to his lips. He knew that the fairy was the girl in his dream and he began to play, to thank her for helping him.

Affirmations

- If you accept an important task, you need to listen carefully to instructions and take responsibility for your actions.
- One good turn deserves another. It's nice to do something to thank someone who has helped you.
- Sometimes it is soothing to clear your mind and think of the gift of water. This is where all life began on Earth.

The Dark
Wood

Relax and empty your mind of everyday thoughts. Be still and listen carefully to this story about a boy and a girl who were very brave.

Calvin loved going with his little sister Kate to visit Grandma and Grandpa in their country home. He loved playing with his football on the long, sloping lawn. He loved watching the woodpecker on the bird table. And he loved seeing the frogs and wriggly tadpoles in the pond.

But Calvin did not like the wild, dark wood at the bottom of the garden. Even on sunny days it seemed black and gloomy, with its long, shifting shadows and strange sounds.

The thought of entering the wood filled Calvin with fear. So when he kicked his football too hard one day and it rolled into the undergrowth, he did not go in and get it. Instead, he sent in Grandpa's old dog, Jet.

One evening before bedtime, Calvin was standing with Kate in the doorway of his grandparents' house, looking out across the lawn. Suddenly he saw a tiny light, flickering and dancing at the edge of the wood.

"A fairy!" said Kate.

"Maybe it is!" smiled Grandpa, as the light vanished. He put his arm around both children. "Tomorrow night I'll take you to see the badger cubs. They live right in the heart of the wood."

Kate squeezed close to Calvin. "I'm not sure I want to go," she said. "But I do like badgers ..."

Calvin liked badgers, too. He thought how very much he'd like to see the cubs. But he wasn't sure he wanted to go into the woods at night either.

"It's all right, Kate," he said, trying to sound brave. "I'll hold your hand. And Grandpa will be there ... and Jet."

"No!" said Grandpa. "We can't take the dog. He'd scare the badgers away."

"Oh," murmured Calvin, who would have felt much safer with the big old mongrel by his side.

"I'll be brave," he told himself. "And Grandpa will be beside us all the way."

All that night, Calvin tossed and turned. His dreams were full of shadows and strange, rustling noises. The next day he felt tired, anxious and cross.

"Ready?" said Grandpa, when evening came.

"Yes!" said Calvin, but his voice came out all squeaky.

Kate nodded her head. "I'm ready, too," she said.

Grandma handed Grandpa a thermos flask of cocoa she'd made for them and waved goodbye as Grandpa led the children into the wood.

The lantern light cast thick bright trails along the path and Grandpa sang a funny, cheerful song about a knapsack as they walked along. The children soon learnt the words and they joined in with the chorus.

"Val-deri,Val-dera,Val-deri, Val-dera-ha-ha-ha-ha-ha ..." they sang.

"It isn't really scary at all, now I am here," said Calvin. But he jumped high in the air when a twig snapped under his foot.

Kate held tight to his hand and kept screwing her eyes tight shut whenever she felt especially scared.

"It's so dark, I can't see," she complained, when she bumped into a tree.

"It's even darker if you shut your eyes," laughed Calvin.

But then something terrible happened. They were close to the place where the badgers might be when Grandpa tripped and fell to the ground.

"Ouch!" he said. He tried to get to his feet, but immediately fell over again. "My ankle is sprained, maybe broken," he told the children. "I can't walk on it. You will have to take the lantern and run back to Grandma for help."

"No!" trembled Calvin. "We can't. Not without you!"

Kate made a small whimpering sound.

"You can do it!" said Grandpa. "Keep the lantern high and follow the path. It will lead you back to Grandma."

Calvin saw Grandpa's face in the lantern light. He was smiling, but his forehead was creased with pain.

"Come on," Calvin said to Kate. "We must get help."

The lantern did not seem nearly so bright now and it was hard to be sure of the right path. Their way twisted and turned, and many smaller tracks led off the main route.

"Which way now?" asked Calvin, his heart pounding as they reached a crossroads.

"Follow the fairy," whispered Kate, tugging at his sleeve.

"We don't have time for games!" said Calvin crossly. "We must fetch help for Grandpa." But as he looked up he caught sight of a small but bright light shimmering among the trees.

For a second he thought he saw a little face and hands, long flowing hair ... and a pair of shining wings.

"It's trying to show us the way home!" he said. The children followed the dancing light as it led them safely along the twisting paths to the edge of the trees.

Grandma called a neighbour and two strong men came to carry Grandpa out of the woods.

"You were very brave," he said to Kate and Calvin. "I'm sorry we never got to see those badgers."

"But we'll go again, won't we?" said Calvin.

"Just as soon as I can walk," nodded Grandpa.

"I hope so," said Calvin. And he knew that when he went back to the woods he would no longer be afraid.

Kate smiled. "And the fairy will show us the way!"

Affirmations

- In an emergency, stay calm and do exactly as you are told. Getting in a panic doesn't help anybody.
- If you feel afraid it helps to know that other people are nervous, too. You'll feel much braver when you are looking after each other.
- Nature should be treated with respect, but there is no need to fear it. Remember that we are part of nature, too.

The Silver
Flute Fairy

Close your eyes and imagine that you are standing in the great hall of a castle. All around you lords and ladies are assembled for a party, dressed in their finest clothes. Women in fabulous silk gowns are carrying brightly coloured fans, and the men are wearing elegant coats and elaborate neckties. On a platform at the far end of the hall, a young princess stands on her own greeting the guests. Even though she is still a young girl, she is smiling and looks confident and relaxed.

This is the story of Princess Tia, who lived in a castle high up on a cliff over the ocean. When she was a baby, her mother and father, the King and Queen, were lost at sea. Princess Tia was brought up by the old nurse who had looked after her mother when *she* had been a little girl. The nurse was part of the family and she loved Princess Tia deeply, but the princess still felt lonely because there were no other children in the castle for her to play with. Her only

friends were the pigs, chickens and sheep who lived on the farm. Princess Tia never left the grounds of the castle and she had no visitors, so she was not used to meeting people.

The princess was approaching her twelfth birthday and the Lord Chamberlain decided that it was time for her to meet her subjects.

"We shall have a splendid party," he said. "Just like we used to have in the old days. I will send out invitations to the most important lords and ladies of the realm. They all want to meet their future queen. You will be the centre of attention the whole night!"

Princess Tia couldn't think of anything worse, but she didn't say anything. She knew it was her duty to attend the party and act like the queen she would one day be.

But the night before the party, the old nurse heard the princess weeping in her bedroom.

"Why are you so sad, my little one?" she asked. "Everyone is really looking forward to meeting you."

Princess Tia looked up and her face was wet with tears.

"Every time I think of all those people staring at me, my heart bangs in my chest and my knees shake so much I can barely stand," she cried. "And when I try to speak, nothing comes out of my mouth." Princess Tia buried her head in her hands. "All those important lords and ladies will think I'm a fool."

The nurse sat down beside the princess and put her arm around her shoulder.

"Be brave, my dear," she said in a kind voice.

As she spoke, she opened the purse she wore around her waist and took out a silver brooch. "Before the party, remember to pin this to the front of your dress," she said.

"What good will that brooch do?" cried Princess Tia, miserably.

The nurse stood up and smiled. "You'll see. Now climb into bed and go to sleep."

As the door closed, Princess Tia looked down at the brooch in her hand. She saw that it was intricately designed in the shape of a tiny fairy with silver wings as fine as lace. The fairy's jerkin was decorated with tiny chips of blue stone and he was holding a diamond flute to his lips.

As Princess Tia held the brooch, the sweetest music filled her head and seemed to spread through her whole body right to her fingertips and toes. For the first time, the thought of the party and all the lords and ladies staring at her didn't fill her with dread.

There was a tinkling sound of laughter. Princess Tia gasped and almost dropped the brooch. To her amazement, the silver fairy was moving! He put down his flute and smiled up at her.

"Don't you worry about anything, Princess Tia," the fairy said. "I'm with you now and you need never feel shy or frightened again."

Princess Tia was dumbstruck! "Who are you?" she finally managed to whisper.

"I'm a fairy," came the reply. The tiny figure held up the flute and waved it at the princess. "Trust me and you'll never be lonely again."

Then he put the flute to his lips and played a tune that sounded like birdsong in the morning.

The fairy stopped playing. "Now go to sleep," he said. He tapped the side of his head with his flute. "And don't forget to pin me to your dress tomorrow."

When Princess Tia walked into the great hall the next day,

she felt like she was walking on air. Her
ears were full of the flute fairy's music. She
wasn't shy or frightened, even for a moment.
All the lords and ladies said how beautiful she was and
how one day she would be a kind and lovely queen.

And best of all, some of the ladies promised to bring
their children to the castle the very next day, so that she
could play games with them.

That night in her bedroom, Princess Tia asked the nurse
about the brooch, but the old lady only smiled a mysterious
smile and refused to explain.

"It's all about love and magic, little one," the nurse said.
"Trust in them both and anything can happen."

As she spoke, the sweet music of a flute filled the room.

Affirmations

- It's normal to feel shy when we meet new people, but remembering the
  good things in our lives can give us confidence.
- If you notice that someone seems shy and awkward, you can help them to
  relax by being friendly yourself.
- An event that you are dreading can turn out much better than you expected,
  so try to be open to new experiences.

Saving a Scarecrow

Close your eyes and imagine that you are lying in the middle of a field of ripe corn, next to a scarecrow. He is wearing an old straw hat and has buttons for eyes. Suddenly you hear a voice. It sounds scratchy, like straw bales rubbing together. It's the voice of the scarecrow!

"Listen to me, child," he says. "I want to tell you a story about a fairy that saved me when no one else could."

You cannot believe what you are hearing. Since when can a scarecrow speak and what is this talk about fairies? You know that fairies only live on the top of Christmas trees …

"Silly child," says the scarecrow, as if he is reading your mind. "Fairies are everywhere." His arm moves in the breeze, showing you the field of ripe corn around him.

"It wasn't always a good crop like this," says the scarecrow. "Pigeons ate the seeds and then crows snapped up the green shoots before they could grow strong."

"Why didn't you scare them away?" you hear yourself ask,

even though it
seems very strange
to be talking to a scarecrow.
"Isn't that what a scarecrow is supposed to do?"

"Of course it is," replies the scarecrow in a
hurt voice. "But the problem was I couldn't see them.
My hat had slipped down over my eyes and there was
nothing I could do about it."

There is a sound like a scarecrow sniffing.

"Then I heard the farmer say I was useless and only
good for the bonfire."

"Oh no!" you cry. "What happened?"

"The hedge fairy saved me," says the scarecrow.
"Look hard over there and you'll see him."

Sure enough, you see a ball of light twinkling in
the tangle of branches! It is bright emerald green and
it's moving as if the fairy is dancing for you.

"Wow!" you cry. "That's amazing!" Suddenly there are
hundreds of questions you want to ask. But when you turn
back to the scarecrow, he is nothing but an old bundle
of straw, hanging limply on the pole. You blink.
What has happened to him? Did you just
imagine it all?

You walk around the scarecrow, examining him carefully from all sides. Then a big smile spreads across your face. His hat is sewn to the back of his head with bright green thread, so fine it looks like a spider's web. And the thread is glowing green just like the light you saw dancing among the twigs.

And that's when you see the hedge fairy! How could you have missed him?

He is tiny and dressed in leaves and swinging on a stalk of grass above the scarecrow's hat. The hedge fairy stares at you with his extraordinary emerald eyes as if he wants to make sure you know he is real. Then suddenly he disappears in a sparkle of sunlight! And all you can hear is the wind rustling in the corn.

Affirmations

- Showing compassion for the creatures around you will inspire other people to behave just as well.
- Sometimes you need to take a second look at things to find out the truth about a situation.
- Instead of throwing something out as soon as it stops working, think how you could give it a new lease of life.

Meditating on Nature

Meditation can be a powerful tool for both you and your child, helping you to process change and difficulties and achieve a calm centre when life is challenging. Nature is a wonderful focus for meditation, offering both comfort and healing.

We are all born with the ability to meditate – you will have experienced its calming effects when you were completely absorbed in doing something you love, such as listening to music. At such times we are taken out of our busy conscious minds, no longer worrying about the past, or what will happen in the future. Instead we are in the here and now, feeling contented, peaceful and at one with the world. By learning to meditate we can bring this same deep focus into our daily life, so that this state of mind gradually becomes second nature to us rather than a fleeting experience.

Choosing a scene from nature as the basis for a visualization-meditation exercise is an excellent way to introduce your child to these skills. Gazing at a beautiful sunset, for example, or focusing on clouds are both absorbing yet restful experiences

in themselves, which can help your child to detach from any nagging fears or anxieties and still a troubled mind.

Try setting aside 5 to 10 minutes each day in which to do a guided visualization-meditation with your child (see pages 136–9 for examples). You could incorporate this into his bedtime routine – either instead of or after reading one of the stories in this book. Speak in a slow, relaxed voice, pausing from time to time to let your words sink in, so that he can follow you easily. It's natural for the mind to wander during meditation. Reassure your child that all he needs to do is return his focus to his body – this could be by doing something very simple such as noticing his breath.

It is important to begin each meditation session by ensuring that your child is in a receptive state to gain the most from the practice. He should be sitting in a comfortable position, with his chest "open", and his back straight so that he can breathe deeply and regularly. If he is lying in bed, be sure that he is lying on his back with his arms loosely by his sides so that his breathing is not restricted in any way. Once you are sure that he is calm and relaxed you can begin.

Sea Fairies Meditation

The fairies of the sea are among the most important of the nature spirits. This isn't surprising when you consider the force of the sea – the pounding of waves against the seashore, the great ocean currents that flow around the continents and the enormous creatures, from sharks to dolphins and whales, that make their home in these waters. The fairies of the ocean realm are strong, independent creatures, long recognized in folktales and mythology. All around the world there are tales of mermaids and mermen, selkies and undines – creatures that often look like humans and may even live with humans on land for a time, but in the end always return to their watery home.

The following visualization-meditation will allow your child to draw strength and courage from the sea world, helping her to recognize her true self. Ask your child to sit comfortably with her eyes closed. Then say:

"Imagine that you are by the seaside in the evening as the light is fading. It is warm, a balmy breeze is blowing and the last light from the sun is turning the sea a gentle lavender colour. Many creatures of the seashore, such as crabs and limpets, emerge at this time when the heat of the sun is lessened and they are safer from birds and other predators. Folktales record how sea fairies, too, gain courage to approach the shore in the evening.

Make your way to the point where the waves are breaking on the beach. You can feel the sand between your toes as the waves gently lap around your ankles. You gaze out to the horizon where the sea meets the sky. The sky is glowing a delicate pink from the setting sun. You see a splash of water. Could it be a fish? But no, it looks like something else — the fish tail of a mermaid! You watch the creature swimming far out to sea, until she disappears among the waves.

Something catches your eye, lying on the sand. It is a beautiful shell, shining like a pearl in the delicate light. You reach down to pick it up, making sure that there is no creature inside — it is important not to disturb the home of a living animal. Lift the shell to your ear and listen to what it tells you:

'You are strong and courageous, like the creatures of the sea. Be yourself and be happy, for you are exactly the person you should be.'

Flower Fairies Meditation

This is a useful guided meditation when your child's spirits are a little low – perhaps he is recovering from illness or having a tough time at school. The message of this meditation is one of growth and rejuvenation.

"Imagine that you are in the middle of a building site. Bulldozers have cleared the ground and all you can see is mud. But wait a minute! An emerald green carpet of grass is spreading out from under your feet in every direction. Daisies are sprouting among the blades of grass, while green stems are pushing up and turning into daffodils before your eyes. And as the flowers bloom, so their fairies appear: tiny white ones for the daisies and sunny yellow ones for the daffodils. Now there are flowers and fairies everywhere: scarlet fairies dancing on the poppies, bright blue fairies hovering above the cornflowers and pink fairies for the carnations. You realize that butterflies, dragonflies and bumblebees are also busy at work. Lie down among the flowers now. Look at the lovely colours, smell the scents of grass and earth, and the sweet aromas of the flowers. Listen to the laughing of the fairies and the hum of the insects. Breathe deeply and feel the energy of spring."

Cloud Meditation

This is a wonderful exercise to calm and help clear your
child's mind. You may like to read this to her in
the morning before school to prepare her for the day.
"Imagine that you are lying in the grass gazing up at the sky.
It is a lovely warm day and the grass smells fresh and sweet.
A gentle breeze is blowing and the clouds above you are
scudding across the sky. Watch as the clouds constantly
change shape. Some are large and puffy, some are long and
stringy, and some are just wisps. As you continue to gaze up,
you see that some are turning into creatures — there is a
curled-up cat, who then stretches out into a giraffe, who
lopes off to find some leaves to nibble on. You can
see the turrets of a magnificent fairy castle emerging,
and its battlements and drawbridge. A fairy princess
is waving from a window in the highest tower. But now the
castle is changing into a forest and you can see an elephant
hiding among the trees. As the patterns in the clouds keep
changing, so each day is different to the one before, and
each minute of each day is different to the previous one.
And today is a completely new day that you are about to
begin. Open your eyes and enjoy it!"

Further Reading

If you and your child become fascinated by the fairy realm, you may like to read more about myths and folktales from around the world. Here are some books to get you started.

Ted Andrews, *Enchantment of the Faerie Realm*, Llewellyn, Woodbury, 2005

Katharine Briggs, *A Dictionary of Fairies*, Penguin, London, 1977

Rosemary Ellen Guiley, *Fairy Magic*, Element, London, 2004

John Matthews and Caitlin Matthews, *The Element Encyclopedia of Magical Creatures*, Element, London, 2009

Teresa Moorey, *The Fairy Bible*, Godsfield Press, London, 2008

Index of Values and Issues

These two complementary indexes cover the specific topics that the twenty stories of this book are designed to address directly or by implication. The same topics are covered from two different perspectives: positive (Values) and negative (Issues). Each index reference consists of an abbreviated story title, followed by the page number on which the story begins.

Acknowledgments

The Publishers would like to thank the two storytellers for writing the tales listed below:

Lou Kuenzler

"The Dark Wood", "The Fairy Trap", "The Fidget Fairy", "Flying High", "Lost in the Fog", "Mia on Mud Duty", "Molly and the Moonlight Fairy", "The Promise of Snow", "A Splash of Fun!", "The Sunflower Race"

Karen Wallace

"The Get-better Garden", "A Light in the Dark", "Nest in the Sky", "A Pearl Ring", "Sandstorm in the Desert", "The Sea Sprite", "The Tractor Fairy", "The Waterfall Fairy", "Saving a Scarecrow", "The Silver Flute Fairy"